Missy and Kobe: A Tale of Two Bulldogs

Copyright@ 2023 by Author: Sue Silverberg, Illustrator: Alex Love

ISBN 979-8-218-16794-3

All rights reserved. No part of this book may be reproduced in any form or by any electronic or mechanical means including storage and retrieval systems without permission in writing from Author: Sue Silverberg, Illustrator: Alex Love.

Printed in United States of America

This is the story of two bulldogs;
Kobe and Missy, two of the world's great dogs.

Would you like to meet Kobe? He is a French Bulldog, also known as a " frenchie." No he does not speak French, but would look amazing in a beret!

Kobe became part of our family two years ago when we adopted him from an animal rescue. Kobe has many health issues. Before we met him he had his insides cut open and part of his intestine removed because it was not working. Now his intestine is short and sweet and helps the food get to where it needs to go.
Know what I mean?

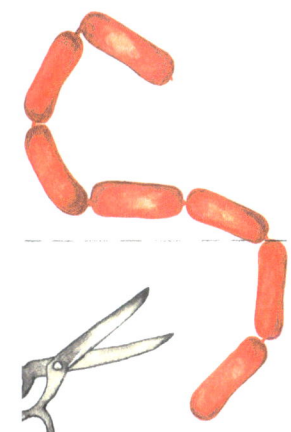

Because of tummy problems sometimes Kobe doesn't feel that well. When he is sick, he likes to sleep up on his perch on the couch where he keeps one eye open, just to make sure he is not missing anything that's going on.

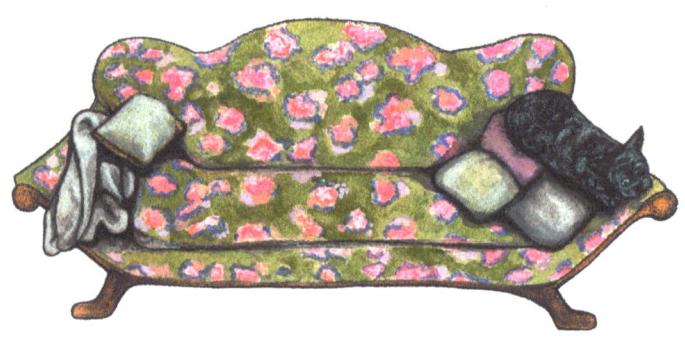

Recently he had surgery on his stomach
which has helped him feel a lot better! Yeah !

Does your tummy ever hurt?
What do you do when you don't feel well?

When Kobe feels fine he loves to eat
and cuddle and play with his sister Missy.

He can go from sitting quietly one moment to racing around
the yard crazily. That's called having the zoomies.

Do you ever get the zoomies?
How do you get your crazy energy out??

Kobe, is an unusual looking Frenchie—he's all spotted with swirls of grey and black and brown. He is so cute you just want to squeeze him. At times he can look like someone else; he can look like a bat,

a piglet,

a leopard seal,(see if you can imagine him looking like a leopard seal) and when he is swimming and sliding along the side of his blue plastic pool—you would swear he is a miniature hippopotamus.

Oh Kobe, you are fantastic!!

Sometimes Kobe disappears and it seems impossible to find him because he blends in so well and does not want to be found. Oh no, Kobe's missing again.

Would you help me look for him?

Can you hide so well that you can't be found?
Where do you hide?
I promise I won't tell!

Kobe is a dog who knows what is most important in the world: Cuddling with the ones you love, a good nap, lying in the sun (or by a heater), eating yummy food, playing with a friend, and cooling off in some water when your belly is hot.

What more is there really?

And now it's time to meet Missy!

Isn't she wonderful?

Missy is an Old English Bulldog.
She's not old—she's five, it's just her breed.
Missy joined our family two months ago when her first family
moved across the country and couldn't take her with them.
She has turned our world upside down in all the best ways.

Missy is very friendly and wiggly and sweet, and has a small nub of a tail that never stops wagging! (Believe it or not some humans cut off dog's tails into a nub because they think it looks better!!!Grown-ups can be weird, huh?)

Missy often looks serious even when she is happy.
Sometimes people says she looks grumpy but this is not so.

What does your face look like?
We all have different ways of looking—and
we're all just perfect the way we are.

Missy has many talents. One of her special skills is
blowing bubbles out the sides of her mouth.

She has fabulous lips!

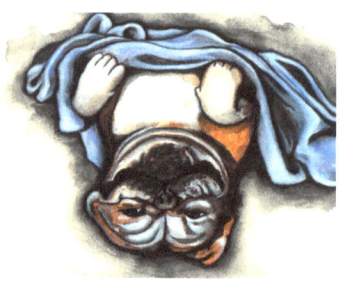

Another cool thing about Missy is that she has a big M on the top of her head. Maybe it's because she's from Missoula, Montana or that she is Magnificent or even Magical?

What do you think Missy's M means?

Do you have any birth marks, or freckles or scars that make you even more special?

Missy, also known as Missy Pooh, Miss Pooh Pooh Nut, and Miss P—loves to run and play and will even throw her own toys up in the air and play catch with herself. Sometimes we need to be our own best friend and Missy is very good at that.

Do you ever feel alone?
What do you do to keep yourself company?

Most of all, Missy loves to have her belly rubbed.
At any moment she will drop to the ground and
show you her tummy and let you know what she wants.

She has the most beautiful speckled belly
that feels silky smooth.

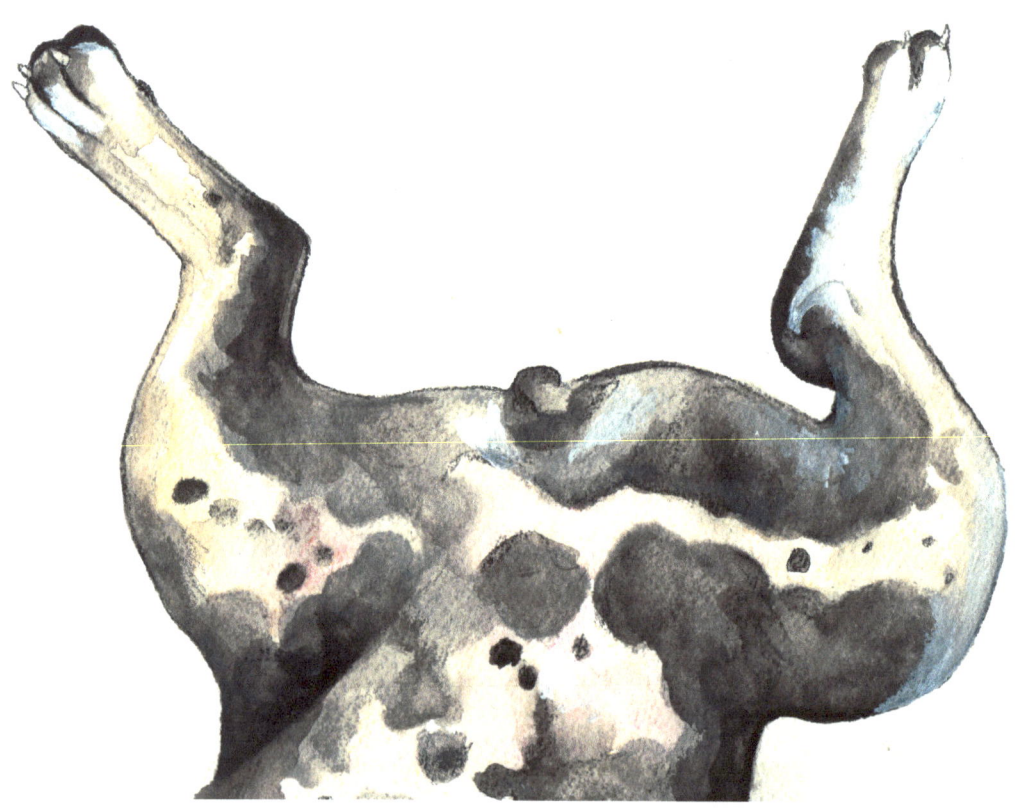

As it turns out, Missy has some health issues too.
She has bad knees.

Bad knee, Bad knee!!!

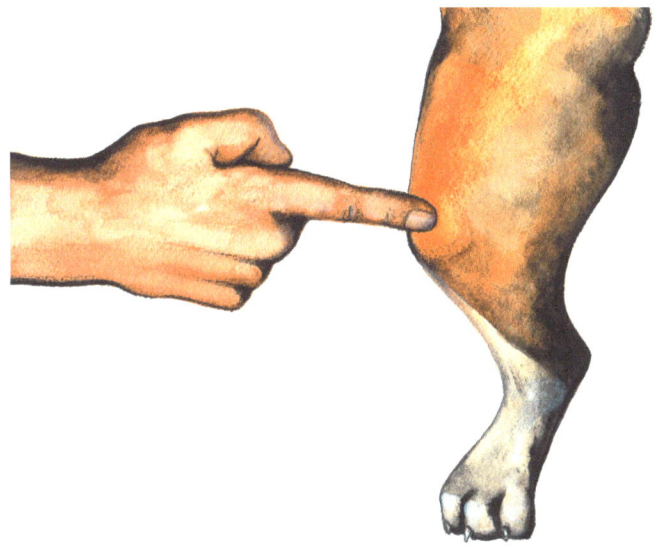

When her knees are sore, Missy needs to rest and take it easy.

Do you have parts of your body that hurt or don't do what you want them to do?
What do you do when you can't run and play?

Although Missy and Kobe have not known each other long, they are the best of friends. They love to wrestle and chew on one another's faces and play tug with their toys.

Sometimes though, they need to take a break from one another when the play gets too rough. Then, it's a good time for a nap.

Here's a few fun facts about Bulldogs. Bulldogs often have smushed faces and flat noses which makes them especially cute and snorty, and snoofly. It also causes them to fart a lot. Just one more thing to love about them! Bullies can also be very stubborn—only listening and doing what you want them to do when **they** feel like it.

Do you know what it means to be stubborn?
It's like standing strong as a tree and not letting anyone else tell you what to do.
Do you ever feel that way?

More fun facts:

Bulldogs have big shoulders and chests and can look kind of tough and mean on the outside but are all sweet and loving on the inside. Their outside toughness is just a way to protect them and make you think they're strong, so that you don't mess with them (a lot like human bullies who try to make you think they're tougher than you, when they're really not!)

Bulldogs are also known for being loyal. This means that once they love you, you will be theirs forever.

Missy and Kobe have some habits that get them into trouble. Kobe is a poop eater. Yep, a poop eater. Worst of all, poop makes him sick, so you can imagine where that leads....
Yuck!!!!!

Missy likes to surf the kitchen counter for treats. Once she ate 2 pounds of raw chicken, plastic wrapping and all. Can you guess what happened next?? YUCK!!!!

Do you have any gross things you like to do? I bet you do!!!!!

Even with those slightly nasty habits,
Missy and Kobe are perfect

JUST LIKE YOU!!!!!

After a busy day of eating, pooping, peeing, running, napping and cuddling, and eating some more, it's time to start getting ready for bed. This is the time of night that Kobe and Missy like to share their thoughts about the day and talk about life's bigger questions....

Kobe would like to share some of his thoughts with you:

"Even though I do love poop, it would be better for my health not to eat it. So please everyone, pick up your own poop (garbage— don't really pick up your own poop) and tell your parents to pick up your dog's poop when you go for walks. If we all cleaned up after ourselves, the earth would be cleaner and my belly would hurt less!!!

And if you don't have a dog friend, tell your parents there are a lot of great dogs who need a good home. You may need a dog friend just as much as they need you!!"

Missy would like to share her thoughts too:

"We dogs just get along for the most part. We don't worry about what breed other dogs are, or what color their fur is—we just accept everyone and are excited to sniff different butts of all sizes and shapes. Maybe you humans could figure out how to do that too and get along.

Also, if everyone just showed their soft underbellies and let them be rubbed when they need a good rubbing—I bet that could help build more kindness and caring in the world. And it would feel great too. There's nothing like a good belly rub.."

And now, it is time for sleep.
Kobe and Missy snuggle into their beds, side by side,
snout to snout, snoring softly—sometimes not so softly—and
dream of great adventures to come.

See you in our dreams!!!

The story within the story

After writing Missy and Kobe, a Tale of Two Bulldogs, I knew I wanted to find someone to draw Kobe and Missy for the book. After talking with a few people and not finding the right fit, I decided to ask a woman named Alex that I met at Missoula's Winter Market—who was selling her beautiful art there. I told her I was looking for an illustrator for a children's book about my dogs and wondered if she was interested. I asked her if she liked dogs as this seemed important. Alex said she did not have a lot of experience with dogs but had fallen in love with one dog over the summer who she had met while hiking. The dog she found was on her own and Alex took her home with her until she could find her family. They spent one special night together and Alex told me she had been thinking about that dog and wishing she could meet her again. She pulled out her phone and said "I keep her photo as the background because she meant so much to me." And there staring back at me was a dog that looked a lot like Missy. I told Alex I was pretty sure that was our dog Missy, and sure enough it was! It turns out that Missy's family before us lived near a hiking trail and let her wander on her own—so that was why Alex found her all by herself.

You can imagine we both had chills about our shared connection to Missy and knew our collaboration was meant to be. Meeting Alex and working together has been wonderful! It confirmed that Missy really is magical and that the story of Kobe and Missy needed to be told.

Alex and Missy reunited!

Sue Silverberg grew up in New York (Long Island) and has lived in Montana for more than thirty years. She lives in Missoula with her partner and two bulldogs and has a son in college in North Carolina. She is a mental health counselor who works with adults. When she is not adoring her dogs, she is often in the garden, biking or swimming in the Clark Fork River. She believes that dogs teach us about kindness and compassion and help us become better people.

Alex Love grew up in Asheville, North Carolina where her grandmother taught her how to translate the beauty of life with a paintbrush. In 2012, she received her Bachelor's degree in Art Management and after years of traveling and living in numerous places, she found herself in Missoula, Montana. Shortly after her move in 2019, she started up ReLove, blending her art with repurposed flowers and other reloved materials. Her mediums range from watercolor, pencil, acrylic, charcoal, oil to ink. These days, you can find Alex and her artwork at the Missoula Farmer's Markets, snowboarding the local mountains or hiking in the sunshine!

CPSIA information can be obtained
at www.ICGtesting.com
Printed in the USA
BVHW012044130423
662336BV00001B/1